The Ghosn Factor

24 Inspiring Lessons From Carlos Ghosn The Most Successful Transnational CEO

MIGUEL RIVAS-MICOUD

MCGRAW-HILL
Singapore Chicago Lisbon London
Madrid Mexico City Milan New Delhi New York
San Francisco San Juan Seoul Sydney Toronto

Published by
McGraw-Hill Education (Asia)
60 Tuas Basin Link
Singapore 638775
Tel: 6863 1580
Fax: 6861 4875
www.mcgraw-hill.com.sg

The Ghosn Factor
24 Inspiring Lessons From Carlos Ghosn,
The Most Successful Transnational CEO

 Education

The Ghosn Factor: 24 Inspiring Lessons from Carlos Ghosn, The Most Successful Transnational CEO is in no way authorized or endorsed by, or affiliated with, Carlos Ghosn, the Nissan Motor Co., Ltd or Renault S.A.

Copyright © 2006 by McGraw-Hill Education (Asia). All rights reserved. No part of this publication may be reproduced or distributed in any form or by any means, or stored in a data base or retrieval system, without the prior written permission of the publisher.

2 3 4 5 6 7 8 9 10 ANL 10 09 08 07 06

When ordering this title, use ISBN 007-124867-6

Printed in Singapore

Contents

24 inspiring lessons from Carlos Ghosn	iv
The five imperatives	1
Generating value	3
Profitability	5
Coaching a successor	7
Keep it simple	9
Vision	11
Looking inside	13
The plan	15
Striking a balance	17
Patience	19
Seize the opportunity	21
Exact measurement	23
Beware complacency	25
Motivation	27
Management engaged	29
Breaking the mold	31
Intensity	33
Stretching the company	35
Implementation	37
Empowerment	39
Priorities	41
Rewarding performance	43
Professional craftsmanship	45
The important little things	47
Key events in the life of Carlos Ghosn	49
Sources	50

☑ 24 inspiring lessons from Carlos Ghosn

Peter F. Drucker published his seminal *The Practice of Management** in 1954, the same year Carlos Ghosn Bichara was born in Porto Velho, then a small developing city along the Madeira River in Western Brazil.

Today, more than 50 years later, it can be said that Carlos Ghosn is the first person truly to embody all the ideas, concepts and principles laid out in that work of Drucker's. Reading it today, one feels almost as if one is reading Ghosn's résumé or list of beliefs and principles, namely that "the work of a manager is to set objectives, motivate, communicate, measure and develop people." That good managers' effectiveness "depends on their ability to get their thinking across to others as well as skill in finding out what other people are after." That a basic quality of a manager "requires integrity of character." Someone who demands "exacting workmanship of him or herself as well as of others." To be able to "give others vision and ability to perform." To emphasize finding the right question rather than the right answer. To be able to see the business as a whole and to understand how dangerous the lack of cross-functionality can be. The realization that "management has to *manage*." That it is not a "passive adaptive behavior; management means taking action to make the desired results come to pass." And the list goes on.

These are by no means new concepts. Indeed, they are the building blocks of any MBA program today but, as Drucker wrote then,

---

**The Practice of Management* (New York: Harper & Row, 1954)

without experience as a manager, "one can learn to recite these things; but one cannot learn to do them." In fact, many large corporations and CEOs have tried to implement many of these concepts, to varying degrees of success. However, as many of us have witnessed in recent years, all too many organizations and managers have depended more on the "rising tide of the economy or industry," and as we have seen, "whoever contents himself to rise with the tide will also fall with it."

It is here that the Ghosn Factor comes into play. What makes Carlos Ghosn different from all the others is that he actually does what he says he will do. He has the ability to analyze and balance the short- and long-term needs. He sets clear and easy-to-understand objectives, and he motivates his workforce to bring results. He believes in total transparency and in constant communication that flows in all directions within the company. He also believes in rewarding contribution wherever it occurs.

In spite of all this, he is the first person to tell you that there is no secret to what he has done or is doing. For all we know, he never read *The Practice of Management.* According to him, he never read any book on management; he learned simply by doing the work. He was running a plant at the age of 26, and at 30 he was placed in charge of Michelin's ailing South American operation. A few years later he took over the North American operation. What is it that drives him and how is it that he succeeds where others have failed? We intend to find out while introducing the man, his words (see the quotes at the end of each chapter) and his work to date.

I hope this will help you make a positive contribution to your organization.

> "I learned the fundamentals of business management from on-the-job experience. And the fundamentals are, well, fundamental."

☐ Make a long list

☑ The five imperatives

Carlos Ghosn is still a work-in-progress. Nevertheless, five fundamentals have guided him and were the basis of his achievements today. Here is what these five imperatives involve.

Clear Vision: By this, Ghosn means a simple direction that management gives to guide the operations of a business. If employees do not understand the priorities, how can they and management work together to achieve them? So vision is essential, and it must be shared and understood across all levels of an organization.

Targets and Commitments: Here Ghosn refers to the necessity of having a clear, articulated and deployed plan. Management is responsible for defining the business objectives and holding itself and all employees accountable for achieving them. These objectives should be measurable and prioritized. And progress toward the company's goals should be communicated often so that everyone knows the business is on course and the rewards for achievement are possible. Ghosn likes to stress the fact that the economy can affect us in many ways, but it does not affect our commitment. If you do not prepare for growth, the growth will never come.

Transparency: This is an important imperative of the Ghosn style of management. In 1999, when Nissan had reached rock bottom, all Ghosn and his team had was transparency. They had to be completely open in order to develop trust, restore confidence and encourage motivation. They put everything on the table, and then worked very hard to deliver results. When performance improved, the results were shared openly in the same manner. Motivation was stirred. Confidence was restored. And trust continues to be built today. Practically speaking, this transparency shows in having a clear price range of products, responding promptly to customers' questions or requests, offering a high level of service or content, knowing the customers and what they want or need. One thing that always pays off in the end is customer service. It is when the products or services are not fully satisfactory that customers start to expect or negotiate a "deal."

Meaningful Marketing with Attractive Products: Attractive products are the keywords here, but marketing resources must be put to good use to emphasize the features and benefits of any particular product and help the customer appreciate that product's unique character.

Performance-Oriented Management: This must take place at all levels of management. If the current situation does not work, action and change are necessary. As the old saying goes, "Even if you are on the right track, you can still get run over if you just sit there." If you are not proactive, you can be certain that somebody else will be—most likely a competitor. Management needs to learn how to do new things rather than do the old things better. And you must remember that competitors are not only *inside* the industry, but they are also *outside* the industry, offering a variety of niche services.

When times are difficult, businesses should not be afraid to benchmark, or take irregular reform measures to build new types of management or new schemes of business that may profit the organization. Ultimately it is the customer who makes the decision on what to buy, how to buy it and from whom to buy it. The customer is becoming increasingly sophisticated, knowledgeable and demanding. If you are too quick to dismiss better ways of doing things, your customers may dismiss you.

> "Focusing on priorities will assure that you are acting on the things that are most important for your organization. If you are doing a good job on something that is not important, you are wasting time, you are wasting talent, wasting energy, wasting resources."

☐ We're just manufacturing products

☑ *Generating value*

Carlos Ghosn talks a lot about value these days. He believes that value is at the core of his message, be it to employees, shareholders or customers. Here is a summary of his message. No matter what the organization's mission, whether you are providing a product or a service, whether you work in a for-profit or non-profit organization, every organization exists to create long-term value for its shareholders.

What does this mean in concrete terms? Simply that you will be rewarded, or not rewarded, based on your organization's ability to generate value. Value can be defined in several ways. In business, value is how we measure almost everything—the benefits, the costs, the performance and the products or services provided. If you are a customer, value to you may mean attractive products and services, a recognizable brand, or a friendly and effective distribution channel. If you are a shareholder, you may value the visibility and transparency of the organization you are investing in, perhaps the attraction of an appealing dividend policy or good returns on your investment, both in the short and long term.

If you are an employee in an organization, then value to you may mean the opportunity to work in a learning environment where you can contribute your skills and enjoy a sense of purpose and fulfillment. You obviously want professional growth, career satisfaction and a competitive level of compensation and benefits.

For an organization's business partners, value may mean working within a clear strategy and developing opportunities for mutual growth and profitability.

For society at large, value exists whenever any knowledge is created, when products or services are developed to maintain the health or support the regeneration of the environment. Value also exists when the quality of life in the communities where we operate is improved. And everyone wants to create the structure, processes, organizational behavior and people mindset that will enable them to create lasting value.

Here are some questions you may want to ask yourself constantly, just as Carlos Ghosn does.

- What do our customers want and need and what is the best way to serve our shareholders? When he announced the Nissan Revival Plan, Ghosn remarked, "There is no problem at a car company that good products can't solve." Give the people what they want. They want products that combine passion, style and performance. And people will pay for something they want.
- How can we become more competitive in our industry and improve how we work with suppliers and partners to assure mutual benefit? You need to have a clear product strategy and product development process. Focus on the customer and not on chasing the competition.
- What is needed to keep our employees interested and involved so that the company will continue to deliver its very best? Keep employees focused on achieving profitable growth. And compensation must be linked to contribution. Ghosn believes that providing employees with an environment that offers training, knowledge and a permanent opportunity to learn and grow is the best investment he knows of, and it is one that will keep value going firmly up.

> "In the world of business, performance is the universal language. If you are looking to national culture for an explanation of a company's failure or success, you are missing the point! A successful business performance in America is measured the same way it is measured in Japan, Europe, China, or in any other market. Quality, cost and delivery mean the same thing around the globe. Everyone counts the same way. The numbers have the same values. At the end of the day, in any time zone, value creation always will be the measure of effectiveness."

☐ Market share

☑ **Profitability**

Carlos Ghosn defines market share as a short-term objective. If market share becomes a long-term objective, it will be easy to sacrifice profit for the sake of market share. When people pursue market share for the sake of market share, they forget to question if the company actually deserves the market share objective it may be obtaining. Market share is or should be a consequence. Market share is a result of attractive products, excellent technology, high quality, cost competitiveness and the total strength of the company.

It may seem obvious that a company exists to make a profit, but more often than you would imagine, a company's decision making is determined and led by other priorities. We should pursue growth, but growth is just a consequence of performance. This does not mean that being productive is all that is needed. A business cannot be cost-effective if it is not productive but it can be productive without being cost-effective. Any decision should be based ultimately on profitability because that is a basic condition for being a good company. For example, if a company's profits drop, then that company most likely will lose its brand power. Consumers will become skeptical and hesitate before making a purchase decision. Soon the company will run out of steam and find itself at a dead end if it pursues growth for the sake of growth alone. It may be offering the customer a good deal, but if it is disregarding value creation, selling something it should not be selling, the result will be growth that it does not deserve.

Before Ghosn's arrival at Nissan, the company often focused on market share and volume to the detriment of its profit objectives. Does this sound familiar? This obsession with market share can lead companies to *buy* market share with incentives. While this may result in a gain in market share, the gain is not deserved, and this practice can and usually does harm the brand over the long term. The focus always should be on profitability or profitable growth. Ghosn has repeatedly stressed the point that profit or the lack thereof is a telling sign. It can tell you much about the health of an operation. The *lack* of profit is like a fever. When your business is not profitable, it is a serious sign that something is wrong. It could be that the products are not right, the marketing is not being carried out in the most efficient way, or the cost base is simply too high, but it does tell you that something is wrong. And as we all know, if you ignore a fever, you can get very sick. In the same way, if you ignore non-profitability, the situation will get worse and the business will suffer.

On the other hand, with profitability one gains the freedom to invest in opportunities, to develop new technology for the future, to create appealing products and services, to attract, retain, train and reward the best talent, to provide returns for shareholders, and to make a contribution to society—all the things a healthy company *should* be doing.

- Focus on profit. If your business is not making a profit, something is wrong.
- Do not focus on market share. Market share is the result of doing the right thing.

"Profit is the reward you earn for doing things right."

☐ Creating a vacuum

☑ Coaching a successor

Once Nissan was back on its feet, Carlos Ghosn had to give serious thought to training the next generation of leaders. Many in the industry believe Ghosn to be an anomaly—not your average business manager—so many shareholders have been concerned about what would happen when Ghosn stepped down. Well, they need not have worried. Leadership training is an innate part of Ghosn's philosophy. He knows that a good leader is not made overnight. He feels that leadership is not something you *do*, but rather an expression of who you *are*.

Ghosn realizes that a leader needs to have extensive business experience; leadership is not something one can learn in a book. One learns by *doing*. And the more difficult the circumstances, the more a person will learn. Challenges teach people what they are capable of doing. People broaden their view when experiencing business in different areas, and in different countries.

Ghosn knows that to a greater or lesser degree everyone in the company looks to the man at the top for guidance and leadership, especially in situations of crisis. No worker, whether American, French or Japanese, accepts token gestures. An executive must be present in the field, especially in the most challenging circumstances, to show people that he or she cares and supports them. Corporate management requires not only decision making but also coaching. Ghosn sees his job as CEO as that of a coach. Coaching is a difficult job that involves giving advice to people. If the company is going to play well and win games for the coach, then the coach must motivate the players, who are the employees in our context. He also has to instill confidence in the fans, these being the stockholders and the customers.

To do his job right, the coach must like his team. The occasional obstacle is simply the flip side of a passion for the company. The relationship must be a total one, not a "work 10 hours, go home and forget about it" relationship, but an ongoing relationship in which the CEO is always emotionally and intellectually connected.

It is also the role of the CEO to shoulder risk. Opportunities for growth can be risks as well. If the results are good, then the CEO is a hero, but if they are bad, then it is the CEO's fault. The CEO is either evaluated highly or not at all appreciated, and not everyone can perform well under this kind of pressure.

People learn from succeeding and failing while working with others. Coaching is like training. In the companies in which Ghosn has worked, he has tried hard to give potential leaders opportunities to recognize their weaknesses and to think about their careers. Those who gain maturity through such experiences will become valuable contributors to the company in the future. How does Ghosn identify new and future leaders? First, the line management will usually make recommendations. For example, an Executive Vice President may recommend a person with high potential in engineering. Once it is confirmed that the person has potential, he or she is assigned to an area where he or she has never worked before. If the person is successful, then management presents him or her with another challenge. The challenges become tougher, and this process continues with other high-potential individuals until the company develops an elite. This elite group has a number of successful experiences that give them confidence in themselves and earn them the respect of their colleagues. Upper management can then choose people for positions based on their contribution to the company, without being misled by which school they may have graduated from or whether somebody personally likes them or not. People will be added or removed constantly from the list of high-potential individuals because few things change as much as a person's potential. They may not all end up as leaders, but it is infinitely better to have 10 candidates for one job than only one or two, and then be able to choose the best person from that list. In the end, the keywords are performance, excellent management skills and trust.

- Train tomorrow's successors today. Do not wait until it is too late. You cannot always expect someone to come from outside to rescue the company when it is in crisis.
- Good leaders are not made overnight. Experience is an essential requirement of a good leader. Remember, leadership is learned by *doing*.
- A good leader has to be a good coach. Leaders need to look at the future while working on the present.

"Good leaders produce more leaders, not more followers."

☐ Complicate the issues

☑ *Keep it simple*

Carlos Ghosn's motto is "keep it simple." Your message should be as simple as possible to ensure that it is understood. If people understand your message, they will act on it. In other words, a business executive who cannot convey his message is useless. Ghosn himself learned this at the Jesuit school he attended in Lebanon. He still recounts fondly how one of his teachers, Father Lagrovole, S.J., taught him the importance of conveying complex things in a simple way, and that having communication skills is an important asset. Father Lagrovole was Ghosn's French Literature teacher and, passionate about his subject, placed heavy demands on his students because he wanted them to share in his enthusiasm and passion. The priest's words still guide Ghosn in his work today, "An amateur attempts to make a problem complex; a professional strives for clarity." Ghosn was only 13 or 14 and did not fully understand the import of what the old man was saying at the time. It was only after years of experience that it became clear to him that the teachings of his old teacher had been guiding many of his decisions along the way. He realized that when he arrived in the United States to take over the job of President in Michelin's North American affiliate. His first speech drew yawns from the crowd and nothing was communicated. He took that experience to heart and made an earnest effort to do better.

As we will see in later chapters, Ghosn knows that the solutions to most problems are quite simple, though most people don't see them because they don't want to see them or are not doing one of the most important things a leader should do to find them, that is, to listen. Whenever Ghosn faces a difficult situation, he first listens. He asks all the important questions but he really listens, and he listens to the people who know best: the employees, the managers, the dealers, the suppliers and the shareholders. A Michelin employee from the early Brazilian days recalled that one day Ghosn reminded her that God had given us two ears and one mouth, meaning that we should spend twice as much time listening as speaking.

It is interesting that this connection between simplicity and listening was reinforced in Ghosn on his first trip to Japan on a visit to Komatsu as a Michelin customer in 1984. It was also his first experience with the Japanese people.

Two things left an impression on the young Ghosn. First, at the meetings, the younger employees did most of the talking, while the bosses listened. Everyone wore uniforms and the casual observer would not have known just by looking at them who held a managerial position. Ghosn was surprised because he knew who the bosses were, as they had exchanged namecards. In France, it was just the opposite. When the boss spoke, the others listened and rarely said anything.

Second, Ghosn was amazed at the simplicity of the factory operations. In Europe, people tended to think that productivity and technology were linked to complexity. In Japan, Ghosn observed for the first time that productivity and technology were linked to simplicity.

He returned to France having learned that you cannot link performance to only one type of solution. Performance can come from different types of solutions. Listening to what customers and employees say is the first step to finding those solutions.

What can we learn from this? Simplicity matters, and to find solutions, one has to listen. But to do this you must be honest and dedicated to the job. You must have a certain amount of passion for what you are doing.

On any new assignment, Ghosn's style is to spend the early days or months moving around and listening to the workers, dealers and customers. He analyzes the past to understand the root causes of problems. Like Father Lagrovole, he is passionate about his work. As the good father told him once, "Unless people infuse their work with passion, they will never get to the core of anything, be it poetry, business, or life."

Sounds simple? It is.

Here are some of the lessons that Ghosn learned from a humble old priest that remain very much alive in the way he operates today.

- Listen first, and then think.
- Express your thinking in the most transparent way possible—and make it simple.
- Never go into a problematic situation thinking you are going to be able to fix it. Ghosn believes that there is a solution to every problem; the key is to extend our antennas to what is happening, understand the situation quickly, find the solution and implement it right away.

"No one is born with great communication skills. You learn only after you listen to people."

☐ "After me, the deluge"

☑ *Vision*

For Carlos Ghosn, a vision is just a picture of how things should look in the long term. It is a perspective that looks 15 to 20 years ahead. One of the big challenges facing the modern auto industry, according to Ghosn, is the management of time. The results of a technological breakthrough, product development or a manufacturing or marketing initiative may not be seen for several years. It is a little like the Pyramids of Egypt; the construction was passed on from one generation of kings to the next, yet each generation knew what it was building. When you are going to begin to build something big, vision becomes extremely important.

Often when giving a speech, Ghosn likes to use a simplified version of the well-known stonecutter story. Two workers are engraving a stone. When asked what they are doing, one of them replies, "I am engraving a stone." The other says, "I am building a temple." And though their answers are quite different, they are doing exactly the same work. Of course you can tell which one had the vision: the first man sees his work only as a chore or something he is obliged to do, while the second one believes he has a mission to achieve a vision. Ghosn often reminds his team, "Don't forget the mission. If you forget the mission, you don't deserve the job."

When Ghosn arrived at Nissan, he soon realized that though the employees were frustrated by the company's poor performance, they had wanted to move forward for many years. They had a sense of where they were, but they needed a destination, a direction for the future.

Unfortunately, these days many employees believe that work is simply a chore to perform in return for a paycheck. The top executive must lead these employees into seeing their jobs as missions, not chores they are forced to perform. The CEO must inspire employees with stories that excite them and make them want to be a part of a similar story.

A clear vision for the future sparks motivation, which drives performance, which leads to results, which feeds motivation, which produces even more performance. We end up with a virtuous circle.

Here are three points that Ghosn likes to remind people who work under him.

- The catalyst for change at any company is the vision.
- People change companies; organizations do not.
- If you think small, you will get only small results.

"The only power that a CEO has is the power to motivate. The rest is nonsense."

☐ **Looking outside**

☑ *Looking inside*

*I*n any company with problems, the easy way out is to blame something or someone for the problems. But this only prevents finding a solution to the problems. When Carlos Ghosn arrived at Nissan, people were blaming Nissan's problems on the exchange rate, on the stagnant auto market in Japan, on the competition, or on other external realities. Ghosn's first mission, therefore, was to get the people within Nissan to realize that the problems they were facing were *internal* problems. There were many dysfunctions in the organization, and these dysfunctions affected every single area of the business. They first had to fix what was wrong within the company. They needed to change the behavior and mindset of the employees, from top management down to the shop floor. Ghosn knew they had to address each problem, one by one, in strict order of priority before they could move on to a higher level of performance.

In times of difficulty, your employees must be behind you 100 percent. In spite of Ghosn's fearsome façade, he has always understood the importance of communicating his message to all ranks within the company and getting their feedback communicated back. The person at the top can see things the people on the shop floor cannot but the workers will not support management when conditions call for stern measures unless they know what is going on.

Ghosn also knew that he had to put forth a clear vision, a direction for the company. He had realized very early in his career that whenever the business ran into hard times almost everyone in the company already knew what the problems were, but what was lacking was a vision of how to get beyond those problems. Having a clear vision shows where you are going, how to get there, and the rewards waiting at the end of the road. Ghosn has learned that the vision must be clear for all to understand and share. He understands that if people don't believe that making changes will improve their situation, then most people will not bother to make the effort to change, never mind going the extra mile. At Nissan, Ghosn had to get everybody to realize that they *had* to change, that they could do much better, and that the result would be a much stronger Nissan that all of them would be proud of and benefit from.

This of course sounds pretty convincing, but at the time Ghosn was being attacked from all sides by critics and skeptics who said, "No, you can't do that!" or "This won't work." Fortunately for Nissan, Ghosn knew that the kite rises *against* the wind, not with it. Nissan was not going in the right direction. It had to go a different way. And Ghosn's vision was its guide.

- First, a clear vision must be built and shared with everyone.
- Second, a credible plan to guide the company must be developed.
- Third, everyone must work to get significant results.

"At Nissan, I am convinced that the motivation of our employees has been the single most significant factor in achieving the remarkable performance that has revived Nissan."

☐ Chaos

☑ *The plan*

Once you have a vision, you need a credible plan to steer your actions. But just having a plan does not mean anything in and of itself. Once you know what needs to be done, you must *act* in a systematic and purposeful way to achieve your goals. Soon after arriving at Nissan, Ghosn put in place what have come to be called Cross-Functional Teams (CFTs). He formed nine teams comprising about 200 key employees, mainly people with high potential in middle management who knew the business well. Ghosn knows that it is not the people in top management who are best suited to challenge the system when it needs to be challenged. The challenge needs to come from all levels of the hierarchy, from people who are willing to challenge the existing situation and, above all, people who are truly competent and knowledgeable.

At Nissan, the purchasing team was made up of people who worked in purchasing as well as people who worked in engineering, in manufacturing and in finance. This cross-functional approach is the essence of Ghosn's management style and the key to his being able to bring about his seemingly miraculous turnarounds. He knows that this approach encourages people to look at situations from different perspectives and experiences. It forces them to look beyond their territorial advantages and more at what will benefit the entire company. If you think about it, everything that the customer asks for is cross-functional in nature, be it about cost, quality or time. Can any one single function deliver this? No. Ghosn has found that the biggest hidden potential of any large company lies at the intersection of the different functions. Unfortunately, this hidden potential is often neglected. It is not really a natural coming-together ground for people. And that is why it is important to institutionalize the concept within a company. If not, then people will naturally shy away from this gray area that lies at the border of their individual functions.

The purpose of the teams was to bring forward proposals and recommendations on what they believed would be the best way to redeploy company resources and revive the company. Ghosn and the executive committee would then react to these proposals, pushing, probing and sending the teams back to dig deeper or to concentrate on other areas. Ghosn would constantly remind them to ask the hard questions, to challenge existing practices and to think in new ways. After three months of intense probing with his CFTs, Carlos Ghosn announced the three-year Nissan Revival Plan (NRP), which consisted of three core commitments: to return to profitability in fiscal year 2000, to attain an operating margin of higher than 4.5 percent and to halve the net automotive debt by fiscal year 2002. These three commitments, of course, involved making hundreds of changes throughout the company in every aspect of the business.

Still, according to Ghosn, coming up with the plan was only about 5 percent of the task. The remaining 95 percent was linked to meticulous execution and delivering the results. Well, Ghosn delivered. Nissan achieved the three commitments in two years instead of three.

- Approach problems cross-functionally. It is at the intersection of the different functions where you will find the greatest potential.
- Act on the plan. Once you know what needs to be done, do it.
- Be willing to change. Challenges need to come from those in the company who are truly competent and knowledgeable.

"A plan has meaning only when it is acted upon."

☐ The bottom line is everything

✓ *Striking a balance*

We all agree that the primary objective in doing business is to create wealth or value. We set priorities, establish objectives and define company strategy, all of which are aimed at sharpening our competitive edge and ability to make a profit. However, in Brazil, as head of the Michelin operation, Ghosn learned that sometimes the chief executive must take his eyes off the bottom line and make decisions based on other factors.

Michelin owned two rubber plantations in Brazil. One was extremely productive while the other was not. However, the latter was extremely beautiful. The productive plantation was flat, with all the trees lined up in rows, totally man-made. The not-so-productive plantation had been bought from Firestone and was completely nature-made. Besides rubber trees, it had many other varieties of trees.

The productivity of the one and the beauty of the other presented Ghosn and his team with a dilemma. How could they make the second plantation more productive without destroying its natural beauty? A team of plantation workers began to study the problem to see if they could come up with a solution. They knew they could never close the gap in productivity completely, but they would try to see how close they could get. In the process of coming up with ideas, they also looked at better ways of using parcels of land that were not suitable for growing rubber trees.

One proposal was to set aside a relatively large parcel of unused land to plant different species of trees and vegetation. Ghosn liked the idea. He likes trees, and he knew that many species were disappearing. They decided to plant every single species of tree native to Brazil on the land.

From the start they knew that they would not be increasing the productivity of the plantation by doing this. But by planting such a large number of trees, they were able to make a positive impact on the weather in the region, meaning more rain and fresher air. Everyone felt good about it, and it acted as a bond between the plantation workers and management.

To this day, that plantation has never reached the productivity of the first one. If Ghosn had based his decision on short-term profitability alone, he might have pursued other means to reduce the cost of the plantation to the company, which might have cost the company in terms of morale. The plantation workers had put their hearts and time into finding ways to make productive use of the land. Planting the trees did not benefit the company in terms of profit, but it helped to preserve disappearing species of trees, and enhance the climate and environment. More importantly, it created strong ties and emotional bonds between the company and its workers. Although intangible, this is a long-term asset. The beauty and splendor of the trees remain, and after Ghosn left Brazil for the United States in 1989, one of the workers wrote him a moving letter saying that they had affectionately called the area "The Ghosn Garden." Ghosn says it remains the best award he has ever received.

- Not all assets are tangible. Some valuable assets are not plainly visible, but that does not mean that they are not there, or that they do not need recognition.
- Look beyond short-term profits. Though short-term profit is often necessary, sometimes one needs to give up something now for a greater return in the future.

"There is a time for everything. I am a firm believer in rational thinking but I have learned from experience that, from time to time, emotions help rationale discover what must be done."

☐ The quick fix

☑ *Patience*

*I*t is perhaps typical of Carlos Ghosn that he learned more about business and management from the actual doing rather than from a textbook. One of his early and important lessons about business came from watching and observing the business and process of producing rubber and the actual cycle of the rubber tree. This opportunity came when Ghosn was sent to Brazil by Michelin to find a way to halt the increasing debt the company was accruing there, and to make the operation profitable. Much of the problem arose from the hyperinflation that Brazil was experiencing at that time, but hyperinflation was not something Ghosn or anybody in the company before had ever experienced. It was a case of sitting down at a restaurant to order and having to pay immediately because by the time the meal was finished, the price would have doubled or tripled. In this chaos, Ghosn looked to nature and the trees he so loves for some inspiration.

Once you decide to start a rubber plantation, first you must buy the land, and then you take a year to prepare the land. Then you plant the seeds. It will take about seven years for the tree to grow before you can begin to extract the *evea*, the white milky substance that is transformed into rubber. You can then use the tree from year seven to year 25 or 26. Then you must cut the tree down and start all over again.

Looking at it from a business perspective, you have seven to eight years of investment, and 18 or 19 years of production before restarting the cycle again. But of course there are always risks involved: disease and the forces of nature. A fire or a serious drop in temperature can easily wipe out years of investment.

Seeing and thinking about all this taught Ghosn the importance of patience. In nature as in business, there is a process and you have to respect that. You can tweak it and make modifications, but once the process is established, the most you can do is try to get through the different steps as quickly and smoothly as possible; you cannot miss or bypass any of the steps. In the course of Ghosn's work experience, whenever he encountered a problem, he started by going through the steps, one by one. Only when you have the products, built up the brand, organized your marketing and sales, motivated your workforce, and streamlined your distribution network can you expect to see a return to profitability or an increase in market share. Like the rubber tree, you cannot take the *evea* from a tree that is two years old. You must wait seven years. It is the natural cycle of nature.

- Be patient. There is always a process behind everything. Follow the steps one by one. If you try to skip any of the steps you will eventually slip and fall.
- Most things must play out their natural cycle. You can try to speed a process up, but you cannot change the nature of things.

"As with the rubber tree, in business there is a time to invest, a time to be patient, and a time for production. There are things that need to be monitored and watched so that you do not lose your investment."

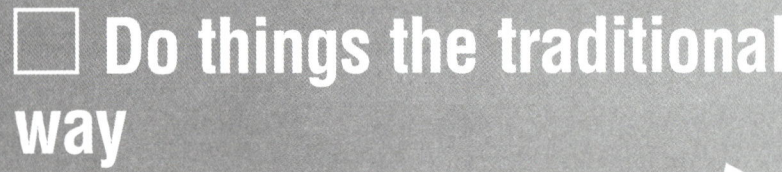

☐ Do things the traditional way

☑ *Seize the opportunity*

Shortly after he arrived in Japan, Carlos Ghosn was asked during an interview what he had wanted to be when he was a child, and he replied: "A teacher." When he was asked what he had wanted to teach, he replied that it was history. As a young teenager, history and geography were his best subjects. In those two subjects he was never beaten in class. When not causing mischief at school, he could always be found with his nose in a book. He was good in mathematics and he was good in science, but his real passion was history. He wanted to be a history teacher. And he once explained why that did not happen.

When he decided to go to university in France, he decided also that he wanted to attend the top business school in France, the Haute Études Commerciales. However, the director of his prep school steered him instead toward the prestigious École Polytechnique, France's top engineering school. He thought Ghosn was too good in mathematics and science to waste his schooling in a business school. That is the French way. Mathematics is at the top of the hill. If you are good at mathematics you must aim for the very best school. Everything else comes after that. And so Ghosn entered the École Polytechnique, though it was not really his decision, but rather a set of circumstances that were beginning to determine the course his life would take.

After finishing his studies there and at the École Des Mines, Ghosn was thinking of a doctorate degree in Economics when he received a phone call from Michelin asking him to join the company. The fact that Michelin had just started its South American operation in Brazil played a large role in his accepting the offer and giving up his plan to continue studying. Eighteen years later, when he had salvaged Michelin's Brazilian operation as well as its North American one, when he had gotten as far as he could go in the company, the offer came from Renault. He explained much later that had the offer come at any other time, he never would have taken it. For one thing, Michelin was not a company that people from management left. It just did not happen. Ghosn himself does not believe in job-hopping, and he does not believe in leaving a job unfinished. He does, however, feel that it is normal and healthy for some people to move once or twice during the course of their careers, but within moderation and for the right reasons. The timing has to be just right.

Often in business as in life, you will find that you start to deviate little by little from your initial objective in the light of opportunities. Ghosn had wanted to be a teacher, started heading off toward business, but ended up becoming an engineer. Born in Brazil, he was attracted to a tire company that was interested in him for a possible future assignment in Brazil. But from an even earlier age Ghosn had been in love with cars, and when the opportunity came to move from a supplier to a manufacturer, everything that he had done till that moment seemed to have trained him for that opportunity. He saw it, took it and we all know what he has achieved with it.

- Have good reasons for the things you do. If you are open to what is happening around you, you will see the opportunities. Big changes may seem daunting, but once you make a decision, stick to it and do not look back.

"Opportunities are always there, even though some people may choose not to see them or accept them."

☐ Have a rough idea

☑ *Exact measurement*

François Michelin put Ghosn, at the age of 30, in charge of the foundering Brazilian operation. This came after six years of moving around within the company in France, working at many different jobs and in different capacities. Looking back, Ghosn says that Brazil was a very important turning point in his professional life. It was not only his first important step into the world of business, but it was a wild environment that was not, nor could it be, readily understood outside.

At that time, Brazil was suffering under hyperinflation at a rate of 1,000 percent per year as well as a very high interest rate (35 percent), which was compounded over the 1,000 percent. Ghosn and his team developed a mathematical model that clarified what measures had to be taken.

- No more servicing of the huge debt. To reduce it, they had to sell off all non-essential assets.
- They could not maintain an inventory as prices were being adjusted all the time.
- They had to demand on-the-spot or even anticipated payments from dealers.
- They had to try to control labor costs by continuous negotiations with union representatives.

These were the measures, but they required constant monitoring. Ghosn realized that a company could collapse very quickly in that kind of environment or it could also rise very quickly. It was a situation where a company could easily end up losing more money than it was making in sales. Ghosn set up two accounting systems, one in Brazilian currency and the other in US dollars, to keep himself and his team from being taken in by the mirage of inflation. Getting back onto the right track required great attention to everything about the business: the stock inventory, timely imports, adequate payments, pricing of products, plant productivity, product quality, union and government negotiations, and workforce motivation—all at the same time. You could not afford to say, "Okay, let's meet again to discuss this next week." When a problem existed, you had to face it and solve it on the spot.

Ghosn says that the most significant lesson he learned at that time was the importance of measuring things precisely, about getting to the core of things without being able to take his time doing so. He had to interpret the figures all the time. He likes to use the analogy of it being similar to looking at reality through a crystal, "You can see only a blur, but you have to systematically reconstitute from the blur what the landscape in front of you *should* look like, or what you should be seeing." And that was what managing in an environment of hyperinflation was like. With inflation numbers rolling at 30 percent a month, without precise and exact measurements you could quickly lose everything. The rigors of that experience forced Ghosn to make immediate decisions based on accurate information. In Brazil, the seeds of Ghosn's management style were planted, and there he matured as a business manager. During his Brazilian experience he realized that the decisions he made affected every employee. It was also his first big turnaround.

- Monitor constantly. Problems can occur at any time. You must monitor what is happening, and when there is a problem, you must face it and solve it right away.
- You need to know the details. Without precise measurement you will not be able to make proper judgments.

"There is no detail in a company in crisis that a president should not know. The president should know of those processes that speed an activity or hinder it."

☐ **Once you make it, relax and enjoy it**

☑ *Beware complacency*

Carlos Ghosn pays attention to the dysfunctions and potential of a company. He has found that there always is a hidden potential in things that are not working well. After a year in Japan, when the situation at Nissan was much improved, he liked to joke that attending meetings that presented him only with good news was boring. Today he usually shortens such meetings to attend those that identify current dysfunctions. Ghosn seems to excel when things are going badly. He seems to see everything clearer when he is at the bottom. After all, there is only one way out, and that is up. He identifies opportunities for improvement, and makes sure that all the employees learn lessons about what should be improved and that they are able to deliver something better the next time. Once a company rises back to the top, things are invariably harder because it is easy to become arrogant, lazy and complacent after success, and that is why Ghosn likes to set tough objectives. He likes to instill in the employees that the objective is to aim to be in the top three companies in terms of quality, technology and operating profit. In managing the people and operations of three large companies and on several continents, he has witnessed first hand the old Druckerism: "… market dominance creates tremendous internal resistance against any innovation and thus makes adaptation to change dangerously difficult."

Ghosn is always on the watch for complacency within the company. He noticed that some people believe that avoiding competition, especially international competition, is the safe way to go. He says that avoiding international competition might be beneficial in the short term, but in the long term it usually turns out to be painful. From the short-term viewpoint, the company will face fewer competitors. But fewer competitors is bad news because it will not force you to change, and it will not force you to abide by the constantly-changing rules by which business is played. With few competitors, a company can easily become satisfied with its performance. When this sort of complacency sets in, a company may not change commodity prices for two, three or even five years. This eventually downgrades the role that the company will play in the market. Ghosn sees complacency as the greatest danger for Nissan today. If management sets easy targets, then they are not really targets. On the other hand, a sense of urgency and a certain amount of risk keep people alert. And by reaching for the impossible, people often actually *do* it. When this happens, the by-products are self-confidence and higher motivation.

Ghosn believes that some people have the latent power to overcome complacency, and it is a leader's duty to draw out that power and unleash the untapped potential of individuals.

- Do not avoid competition. Avoiding competition will only hurt you in the long term, however beneficial it may seem at first. Pressure from outside will force people to change, make progress or improvements.

> "Challenging objectives are weapons to avoid complacency and arrogance."

☐ If it isn't broken, don't fix it

☑ *Motivation*

Most of us would not disagree that the main asset of almost any company is people. But the important question is: "How do you make this asset beneficial for the people themselves and the organization to which they belong?" This is a great challenge that has caused many a CEO to lose his or her footing.

Carlos Ghosn feels that the first important step is to get the people motivated. They should dream of adventure, the vision thing, the destination and all that they want to realize with their lives. When speaking, Ghosn likes to quote the words of Antoine de Saint-Exupéry, the French pilot and poet who once wrote: "If you want to build a ship, don't drum up the people to collect wood and don't assign them tasks and work, but rather teach them to long for the endless immensity of the sea." It is, after all, the workers who must build the ship and the employees who must carry out the necessary changes within an organization to make it profitable. And how do you do it? You do it through motivation. The people must be motivated. They must perceive clearly their visions of what they want to realize for their family, town, company or country. They need to know what they should do today and tomorrow to make their dreams a reality. But motivation, like trust, is not something you can command. It is a very personal response that people offer ... or don't. If people are motivated, everything else will follow: wealth, sales, profits and loyalty. If they are not motivated, then you lose everything. An organization can have the most brilliant strategy but if its employees are unable or unwilling to understand the strategy, then can we say the strategy is good?

In practice, how does one motivate a large workforce? People need to have a sense of participation. Like the stonecutters, if they feel that they are doing enough to get by, then you have not motivated them. During the Nissan Revival Plan, motivating the entire workforce involved sharing the vision, building credibility, listening and showing trust. Most importantly, management could not falter or compromise. Ghosn knows that you must lead by example, no matter how difficult the decisions you must make. He knows that words are cheap, and though people may listen politely to what you say, what counts is what you *do*. Perhaps more than any other corporate leader today, Ghosn has seen that one can accomplish many things that are difficult or that people say cannot be done, as long as one holds the minds and hearts of people to inspire them to go the extra mile.

But motivation works both ways. Ghosn has always given credit for past successes to the employees of the companies where he has worked. He may have been the leader but he never would have been as successful as he has been without having been supported, helped and motivated by his employees.

Ghosn believes that management's first priority is to establish a clear vision and a common long-term plan for the organization. A clear vision will determine strategies, guide action plans, direct performance and boost the motivation of all the people involved. Focused performance will produce measurable, positive results, which, in turn, encourage motivation, confirm unity of purpose, and prompt better performance.

Here are three ideas that Ghosn likes to remind himself and the people who work with him.

- When people are motivated to perform, they can achieve remarkable things.
- Great people are just ordinary people with an extraordinary amount of determination.
- When ordinary people are determined to overcome their difficulties and prove what they can do, the results can indeed be great.

> "There is no secret formula for corporate revival, but there is one common denominator, the motivation of the people."

☐ Hiding in the wings

✓ *Management engaged*

Carlos Ghosn recounted his very first lesson in management, or perhaps we should say mismanagement. He started out at Michelin in the Michelin way, which was the same for everyone, no matter who they were or what university they had graduated from. After a short initiation stage, they all began work on the shop floor. Many of them knew perhaps that their future lay in the executive ranks but they also knew that it would happen only after they had put in their time working shoulder to shoulder with the workers.

Ghosn was assigned to a factory in Le Puy, near Clermont Ferrand, and he had to wear the same blue uniform that all the workers wore. He also had to work all three shifts. At first he was put to work with an elderly fellow whose job was to teach Ghosn about the equipment and the work to be done during each shift. Ghosn's job was to help the old fellow. The man had no respect for the factory rules, and would often smoke on the shop floor. He told Ghosn on his first day that one of his important assignments was to keep an eye open for the supervisor. He would need time to put out his cigarette. Ghosn soon discovered, however, that the supervisor rarely came into the shop. Usually he would come only once in a shift of eight hours to check on production. The result was that the workers could figure out when the supervisor was coming and would organize their work around his expected arrival. More of a surprise to Ghosn was that the plant manager would make even fewer appearances on the shop floor. When he arrived, it was like getting a visit from the Pope! And all this taught the young Ghosn an important lesson. He began to see the differences in the perception that management had of conditions on the shop floor and the reality of those conditions. Ghosn started to wonder about the meaning of having rules if they were not going to be followed. What was the meaning and added value of management's role in the business? The workers seemed to be acting out the roles that they had been assigned without questioning what they were doing or why. And there was little or no training or coaching by management, and no challenges. But there was a desire to get ahead.

As part of his training, he was assigned an instructor whose job was to give him technical information about the different equipment in the shop, and to teach him about the procedures and rules of the factory. Ghosn would meet with him for one hour after each shift. One day, knowing of Ghosn's background, the instructor asked Ghosn to teach him mathematics. He wanted to move up in the company and thought that if he brushed up on his math skills, it would help. So Ghosn agreed to tutor him. His one-hour session then turned into 30 minutes for Ghosn and 30 minutes of math for the other fellow. This revealed to Ghosn that there was a thirst for knowledge among the workers within the company but it was not noticed or acted upon by management. He saw how highly motivated workers could become if given the training that would help them move ahead.

The gap between management's perception of the shop floor and the reality created an artificial environment as far as Ghosn could see. As long as the supervisors and managers were not a visible part of the picture workers were painting for them, then management would continue to receive an incomplete picture of what was going on. The result was that they would never be able to measure with accuracy the productivity of the shop. And without accurate measurement, they would never be able to implement effective steps to improve competitiveness.

In times of crises, however, without honesty and transparency, people will get nowhere. Ghosn has a little story he used to tell in the early days of the NRP.

Two men—Pierre and Hiroshi—go moose hunting in Canada. They hire a small plane to take them to their destination. They go out hunting and bag an extremely large moose. When the pilot sees the size of the moose, he says, "Hey, that moose is too big to put into the plane. We'll never be able to take off." Pierre says, "Don't worry! We did the same thing last year and the plane took off." So they load the moose onto the plane. And they manage to take off, as Pierre had assured the pilot.

But a few minutes later, the plane begins to sputter and then crashes in the woods. Luckily, no one is injured. They get out of the plane, and the pilot asks, "Does anyone know where we are?"

Hiroshi looks around and studies the terrain. Then he says, "Yes. About 500 yards from where we crashed last year."

The moral of the story is, if you are not honest and transparent and try to hide problems, you will not solve anything, nor will you avert catastrophe. Bring the problems out into the open, discuss them and find solutions to them. And that is what Ghosn has done from the very beginning.

- Make everything transparent. Management must know what is happening on the shop floor, and people on the shop floor need to know what is going on in the rest of the company.

"There is no magic. There are no tricks, and there is no secret. The results are the outcome of a credible plan, determination, focus, discipline, and swift execution."

☐ Don't rock the boat

☑ *Breaking the mold*

Carlos Ghosn often brings up the subject of CFTs or Cross-Functional Teams, and indeed he often credits these teams for his success so far.

He first made use of the concept in a systematic way between 1992 and 1996 while at Michelin, North America. However, the concept was still in its infancy, and he had to develop the guidelines and procedures from scratch to implement them. Michelin had just acquired Uniroyal Goodrich and it was Ghosn's job to create a single management team that would supervise all the restructuring and reorganizing needed to move from a strong one-branded global company to a multi-branded strategy for the Michelin, Uniroyal and BF Goodrich brands. This involved, among other things, closing plants, distribution centers and reducing headcount as there was a lot of overlapping between the different organizations. Ghosn had to implement these measures when the US car market was faltering, and the US and Europe were going into a recession. At first task forces were put into place but, as usual, single functions only talked to their counterparts. Finance people talked to finance people, marketing people talked to marketing people and, as Peter F. Drucker pointed out in 1954, they ended up with "a loose confederation of functional empires, each concerned only with its own craft, ... each bent on enlarging its own domain rather than on building the business." Ghosn had already witnessed this in Brazil, but because of the sheer lack of time there, he literally had to force people of different functions to sit down and talk to each other.

In North America, Ghosn knew he needed to do better. He needed to challenge the ways things had always been done. And the crux was that they could fix nothing by working function by function.

The CFTs would have to become a company process, a process to be implemented. And so the first CFTs were formed and he brought people from marketing and sales, R&D and manufacturing together and said to them, "Look, we want to maintain quality, but also make sure that the specs we are building are related and necessary." After all, there is such a thing as redundant quality. He put purchasing people together with engineering and logistics and asked them questions like: Why do we need 80 percent natural rubber? Considering the cost, can't we use a little more synthetic rubber? Do we need to use the highest-grade natural rubber? Can't we mix in a little second or third grade rubber? Will it make a difference to the quality of the product? These questions had never been asked before but you could not ask them and expect a serious answer without having a cross-functional team, which could give you all the angles to a particular question. With a CFT you could get the inside track right away on what the customer thought and what the manufacturing people or the purchasing people thought.

Ghosn learned a great deal about how to marry two different cultures, not only the French with the American, but also the Michelin culture with that of Uniroyal Goodrich. And here Ghosn got his feet wet managing a cross-cultural operation, an experience that would play a significant role years later when he landed in Tokyo. For it was at Nissan where the CFT reached full maturity. Ghosn today says that the idea can work only when you are ready to challenge any preconceived ideas that might exist, his famous "changing of the mindset." In fact, when he established the nine cross-functional teams at Nissan in July 1999, each team had one rule: no sacred cows, no taboos, no constraints and no cultural cop-outs—Japanese, European or North American.

- Challenge the old ways. Have people of different functions talk to each other. No problem can be fixed when working solely function by function.

"Competing in the global marketplace requires the contributions of multi-talented, multi-cultural people working together to achieve success."

☐ Lack of concentration

☑ *Intensity*

Judging from the nicknames Carlos Ghosn has picked up over the years (Cost Killer, Ice Breaker, Mr. Seven Eleven and Turnaround Artist), it would appear that many people have the impression that the man works well only in a crisis. Some suggest that if there is no crisis he is not interested. This does not really do the man justice. Obviously he is not afraid of challenges, and he manages himself well in a crisis situation, but even when things are running smoothly, Ghosn likes to create an atmosphere of urgency—even though outwardly the situation does not warrant such urgency. He does this to make sure that people are working on priorities. He admitted once when pushed on this issue that it is true that when he was not in control of the situation, when, for example, he was dealing with a management that was rather relaxed, and when he didn't feel he was being used to his full potential, then he could get bored.

Ghosn is an intense worker. He tends to get bored when the work or challenge is not intense. However, this does not mean he requires a crisis because, according to Ghosn, you can create intensity in a situation of non-crisis, for example, by creating new levels of excellence or new challenges within the company.

Just before Ghosn moved from Michelin to Renault, Louis Schweitzer, the CEO of Renault at the time, had embarked on a company plan that called for a cost reduction of FFr 3,000 per car. Shortly after Ghosn joined the company, he came up with a plan that went far beyond that: a whopping FFr 20 billion cost-reduction plan over three years. Almost everyone laughed him off, saying he must have tacked on one too many zeros. Many thought he was living up to the first nickname he was given after joining Renault, "Martian." That was how the newspapers portrayed him at the time, "Carlos Ghosn is a Martian!" Fortunately for the company, his plan was not blocked. It was greeted with much skepticism and rumors of his impending fall from grace but he was allowed to run with it. Ghosn himself was becoming familiar with the pattern by then. When you formulate an aggressive plan, you are bound to meet with skepticism, but when you start to implement the plan and show results, people start to change their reactions from "He'll never get away with it" to "Well, this might not be so bad after all." Gradually you win over the skeptics and turn them into supporters. This in turn builds momentum until you end up with anticipation.

Ghosn pulled that plan off. It started in 1998, went on through 1999 and 2000 and at the end of 2000 it was reported that the books showed a cost reduction of more than FFr 20 billion.

- Attack the priorities. Put your house in order, find and work on the core issues first.
- Create intensity. You can always create intensity even when things appear to be going smoothly. Think of new challenges or levels to reach for.

"Creating intensity has to come from the top."

☐ Let things be

☑ *Stretching the company*

Management is always aware of problems but what at times slips by unnoticed by top management is the seriousness of a particular problem. When that is discovered, it can come as a surprise.

For example, the lack of cross-functionality within Renault was obvious to Carlos Ghosn the moment he arrived. People were not working together and this was hurting the company. But then cross-functionality, or the lack thereof, according to Ghosn, is the main problem within the entire car industry. He had already noticed this as a casual observer dealing with his Michelin customers in North America, but when he came to Renault he saw how big a problem it was. Later, when he moved to Nissan, he witnessed the same thing.

A major problem with the people at Renault, a very rigorous group of people—and Ghosn believes this may have something to do with French culture—was that they did not like surprises. The result is conservatism, which leads to a lot of potential never seeing daylight. This is an example of how culture can lead you to be conservative and totally reasonable in all the goals that you set yourself. But when you set yourself only a conservative goal, it is all you will end up achieving. The whole potential of the company is neither unleashed nor stretched. This is totally contrary to Ghosn's management philosophy and experience: he believes that a company needs to be stretched, that people need to grow and that you need to be a little aggressive. Not so overwhelmingly aggressive to leave you short of your goal but that the stretch itself is a normal part of the process.

The solutions to problems are often known but seldom brought up because everyone is afraid of being a victim of any possible change. Often a plan is begging to be conceived and formulated. For example, before Ghosn's arrival at Nissan, production lines had been closed but not plants. He sees this as the wrong kind of compromise. You may reduce some of the problem and some of the cost but not all of it. It is like taking cough medicine for a throat tumor that should be removed. You may feel a little better for a short time but you are not curing the disease. And everyone knows that the problem is not solved. So workers become anxious again and start to worry about their jobs. There begins a vicious cycle. At times like these it helps to have an outsider evaluate things. The outsider (and by this Ghosn does not necessarily mean a foreigner) does not bring with him preconceived ideas about the company, which is an advantage. He can see clearly, while those inside the company may have become so confused about tradition and relationships with people that they lose track of priorities and responsibilities. An outsider can reorder priorities and cut through entrenched procedures that are redundant and wasteful. At Renault in France, everyone had known that one big problem was over-capacity. It had been clear for a long time, but until Ghosn joined the company the decision to close a major plant was not brought up or acted upon. When the decision was finally taken, it caused an uproar in Europe, but in retrospect it was a major factor in the tide turning in favor of Renault, and was a model for what would come at Nissan.

- A company needs to be stretched. People need to grow and management sometimes needs to be a little aggressive.

"I have learned that when you have to make a painful decision, it is better to do it quickly and decisively. Procrastination only prolongs the pain."

☐ The idea is everything

☑ *Implementation*

Carlos Ghosn has always been convinced that implementation is everything. The idea is worth perhaps only 5 percent, 4 percent or even 3 percent. Whether the idea is good or not may well depend on how it is implemented. The same idea might have been tried a few years before with disastrous results. Nevertheless, this does not mean that the idea itself is not good, but possibly that the implementation was wrong.

To be able to make the changes needed and to get employees behind any reforms, one must be able to get into the psychology of the company. Every company, like a human being, has its own character, personality, experience and psychology. The modern term is corporate culture. And Renault in 1996, as Ghosn saw it, was a company with a lot of questions about its future. People were obviously challenged by the fact that there were some problems with sales, mainly because the cars were very expensive. And though this was obvious, people were not confident about how to get out of this situation. Fewer sales lead to higher costs, and higher costs lead to fewer sales. So how do you get out of this vicious cycle? These were the questions facing Ghosn when he arrived at Renault. Renault was still stuck in the European market, and had suffered two bad experiences recently, in its bid to buy Volvo and its attempt to enter the US market. Both had failed miserably. These experiences created a negative mindset among the employees and left them somewhat shaken and less confident about the future.

Yet there was no dearth of solutions from employees. In fact, there were a lot of good ideas that the company eventually ended up implementing successfully later on. These were ideas that had been tried in the past but had not produced the desired results. When

Ghosn entered the picture and offered suggestions and asked about certain previous plans, many people would stand up and say, "But we tried that already three years ago, and it was a disaster. It didn't work."

Ghosn came to the realization that there was the impression in the company that the idea alone, or just the idea of progress, was as important as the progress or implementation itself. For many, the idea was even more important than the implementation. In this situation it was necessary to convince everyone that it was worth trying again, but this time in a different way. This time the implementation was going to be monitored, measured and deployed to achieve the desired results. It was. And it worked.

- Try the plan again, another way. Never give up on the first try. The idea might have been good, but simply not implemented in the right way.
- Implementation is everything. How you do things can change everything.

"Our plan became credible when it delivered meaningful results—results you could see on the shop floors, in our showrooms, in our research centers, and in our balance sheets."

☐ Total control

☑ *Empowerment*

Shortly after Ghosn arrived in Japan to take over as COO of Nissan, one of the first obstacles he faced was the traditional Japanese seniority system. Everything about it ran against Ghosn's experience and beliefs. He strongly believes that such a system stifles performance and innovation by protecting or isolating people from competition.

Ghosn thinks much talent has been wasted and many opportunities missed because of preconceived ideas about age. He believes that what counts is maturity, not age. And we all know that you can have older people who are immature and mature people who are very young.

When talking about his past, especially setting off at the age of 30 to take over Michelin's South American operation, he likes to compare it to being presented with a beautiful sailboat and told, "There is the stormy ocean in front of you. You can do what you want with the boat. If you want to hug the shore, you can, but if you want to set sail in uncharted seas, you are free to do so. It is up to you."

Ghosn says that the beauty of being young and being faced with a challenge is that one is full of energy; one doesn't stop to worry too much about the seas, the storms and the waves. Just cast off and sail away. But Ghosn stresses an important point here: one needs to know how to sail a boat. Without that knowledge, it would be almost like committing suicide. But as Peter Drucker pointed out, it is essential not only to have had experience as a manager but also experience as an adult. Character and integrity are indispensable ingredients a person must bring to the job.

It is a difficult balancing job, on the one hand empowering people with responsibility to go out, make their mistakes and learn from them, and on the other hand giving them enough time to get ready for a difficult assignment. Without making mistakes, they will not learn how to spot mistakes quickly enough or how to correct them when they do spot them. However, if people are pushed too early into a tough situation for which they have not been sufficiently prepared, it can greatly undermine their confidence and future performance. It is similar to raising children. Do you micromanage or not? Ghosn refuses to micromanage because he is sure that it is debilitating for people and for performance. He was very much helped by being put very young and very quickly into a situation where François Michelin told him he was in charge. "I know you can fix it. Go and fix it. If you need my advice, I am here, but you know what to do." Ghosn learned from this that when you put people in a situation where they put the pressure on themselves, it is much more challenging than any pressure that may come from outside, that "nothing challenges people as effectively, or gives them more pride as a job that makes high demands on them."

Ghosn's experience at Michelin convinced him that this was the appropriate way to manage. Strategy must be centralized, guidelines or standards must be established, critical objectives must be established, globally or centrally, long-term and business plans established once and for all, but then you should let the people run with it. Do not micromanage and look over their shoulders. If there is any big deviation in performance you will need an explanation, but if things are moving along smoothly, people should not be micromanaged. Give them space and give them trust. This is the best way for them to achieve. However, Ghosn is not advocating free and unencumbered empowerment. There must be guidelines, priorities and critical objectives to guide the activities and behavior of everyone in the company. Without a clear strategy, clear guidelines or clear priorities, you end up with each person heading off in his or her own direction. Management must, therefore, dedicate a lot of time to selecting the right people, a lot of time to strategy, to critical objectives and business planning. But that's it.

Here are two points to remember.

- Shed all preconceived ideas. Always start with a blank sheet of paper.
- Do not micromanage. Give employees room to make their own mistakes. Coach and support them, but always give them enough leeway to maneuver on their own. Once they are ready for the job, let them run with it.

"I will always remember François Michelin as the man who stood behind me and encouraged me to accomplish what other people considered to be impossible, and fundamentally who always gave me the impression that he trusted me more than I trusted myself."

☐ Indifference

☑ Priorities

Confusion within a company is a sure indication of mismanagement. And confusion usually appears when people do not have clear ideas about what the priorities should be. This is the situation Ghosn found on his arrival at Nissan. He recalls, "It was as if people were mixing apples with oranges, diamonds with stones, and giving them equal importance. It was a pity to see how much wasted effort had taken place for so many years."

It is the responsibility of management to develop the potential of the company. Management is about the company, it is about the people and it is about the situation the company finds itself in. Management's job is to get the most out of the company and its people.

Management's job also is to set the priorities. Anyone who has ever worked under Ghosn will tell you that his management style is easy to follow and consistent. The reason for this is that he establishes clear guidelines and he sets priorities. In other words, he puts apples with apples and diamonds with diamonds.

It is essential to establish the priorities and the objectives you want to aim for. You have to look at your profit and loss sheet to see where the core problems are. If the cost of purchasing is 60 percent of your costs, then something must be done about it. With the recognition of the problem comes development. You start building a plan from the ground up. Priorities, organization and execution of the plan are key elements in revitalizing a company.

At Nissan, Ghosn told everyone that the first priority was purchasing. Unless they addressed that issue, all cost cutting on peripheral issues like telephone or air-conditioning bills, and cutbacks in employee perks would mean nothing. He told them not to spread themselves too thinly, to focus on the major issues and find the solutions for them first. Top management had the responsibility for determining the order of the priorities and of ensuring that the top priorities were followed.

That is how he was able to dismantle the traditional Japanese *keiretsu* system. Whenever someone argued that Nissan was obliged to maintain the old cozy relationships with its suppliers, Ghosn would counter with a simple question: "Where is the justice in doing that?" He felt it was wrong that the company was cutting the salaries of the directors because of the company's poor performance and that employees had to lower or turn off the air-conditioning to save on electricity bills—all in order to maintain a cozy relationship with a supplier that was charging 20 percent more than what other automakers were paying for the same parts. In effect, these measures ended up punishing the workforce and they did not attack the real issues. It made no sense from a management point of view. Lowering the air-conditioning by one degree and other similar cost-saving measures skirted the issue of establishing priorities and reducing the cost of purchasing. If the issues at the core of the company's difficulties are not addressed, the company will never pull out of a financial morass. It is management's job to look at priorities and understand what the solutions are. And by the way, Nissan employees are once again enjoying their perks.

- Clarify what the priorities should be. Everyone in the company needs to know what the priorities are and what objectives need to be achieved.

"When you are in a position of responsibility, you have to begin with a lucid assessment of the way the situation is, not the way you want it to be."

☐ **Seniority rules**

☑ *Rewarding performance*

*P*eople need a certain amount of self-control—in this case control over their own performance. This type of self-control always leads to stronger motivation, which in turn leads to a desire to do one's best rather than just enough. But to do this a worker needs to know more than what his own goals are. All workers need to have clear, simple and rational information against which to measure their own performance. And, of course, people should always be held accountable for the results of their performance. Knowing they are accountable makes them more responsible, and responsibility will lead to authority. Ghosn has found that people with authority usually deliver. And when they do, they must be recognized, encouraged and rewarded, regardless of their age, education or background. We can and should build only on strengths, not on weaknesses. People achieve things by actually doing them, and so an effective appraisal system must be in place that aims to bring out what people can *do* rather than to emphasize what they *cannot do*. Rewards then can be tied directly to the objectives that have been set. But it is also important to remember that not all contributions to the organization will yield precise and measurable results. Some people and their work create strong ties and emotional bonds between the company and the workers and within the management team. Although intangible, this is a critical long-term asset. These contributions may still be important for building vision within the company. These contributions also must be noticed, appraised and rewarded.

At Nissan, Ghosn implemented a system for compensation and promotion. There are clear criteria that are tied to achievement of commitments and targets. This incentive system includes stock options, a bonus system for managers based on achievement of personal and company objectives. Promotion is based on competence and track record regardless of age, gender or nationality, and a nomination advisory committee was established. In top management, whether in Japan or outside Japan, no promotion is approved without a review of the candidate's specific contribution to the performance of the company. With this new performance-based management system in place at Nissan, Ghosn believes that employees now can more clearly see constructive methods of achieving their goals. So far it seems to be working very well.

- Build on strength. Reward those who do well. People need to be motivated in order to work harder.

"Having performance-based compensation and career advancement creates a healthy workforce because it rewards people for the contributions they make, their worth no longer being defined simply by age or gender."

☐ **All you need is an MBA**

☑ **Professional craftsmanship**

As we near the end of the book, it is perhaps a good time to ask what makes a company excellent. Carlos Ghosn believes that an excellent company is one that enriches all of its four main shareholders: its stockholders, customers, employees and society. This involves both long-term strategy and short-term results. You cannot manage with just one or the other. You must strike a balance between them. According to Ghosn, an outstanding company is one that achieves good short-term results while taking matters into consideration from a long-term perspective. And how do you keep this balance? Reading the latest business or management book is no guarantee for success. In every situation you need to make your own judgments, but you must always remind yourself that you are in business and you must learn that decisions cannot be influenced by emotions. Emotion is something personal. It is not professional. Showing emotion is not the job of the president. Decisions can be based only on the creation of value and on priorities. You must balance the long and the short term, and your business must create benefits for the company and for society. It is something Ghosn likes to call "professional craftsmanship." He does not believe that there is any such thing as a universal system, or a system that will work every time in every situation. And what that means is that management must always be on its guard and able to shift with each new set of circumstances. Management must always be flexible and on the move.

However, there are some things that do not change—a person's beliefs and values. These do not, and should not, change. When a person is facing a tough situation, and there is nowhere to turn, no manual in which to seek directions, then the only thing left to function as a guide is the person's values and beliefs. Without these, it is like being in a rudderless boat out on the sea, totally lost without a compass.

Harnessing one's knowledge and experience to one's values and beliefs to create something new is, to Ghosn, the essence of professional craftsmanship. And the presence of professional craftsmen in an organization will determine whether society looks up to it or down on it.

- Aim to enrich the four main shareholders. An excellent company takes care of its stockholders, customers, employees and society.
- Decisions should be based only on value creation and priorities. Emotion is personal and should not get in the way of the important decisions.

"When Nissan selected me to head the company, they hired me to fix the problems. They told me to revitalize the company and to save it from bankruptcy. They did not expect me to display emotion or to agonize over the decisions I made. They hired me to safeguard the company."

☐ **The little things**

☑ *The important little things*

*O*nce during the height of the implementation of the NRP in the summer of 1999, Ghosn was sitting in the company cafeteria eating a Japanese-style lunch. He was determined to eat his Japanese food with chopsticks, though at the time he still lacked finesse. He was holding the chopsticks close to the bottom of the sticks, struggling to clasp the rice and bits of food.

As he was eating, Yoshifumi Tsuji, the former president of Nissan (1992–1996) and at the time an advisor to Nissan, was sitting in front of Ghosn and observing his inept handling of the chopsticks.

"Ghosn-san, hold the chopsticks like this," he said. Ghosn watched him hold up the chopsticks with his hand and fingers in the proper position. "Like this!"

It surprised Ghosn that an advisor to Nissan would spend so much time instructing him on the proper method of using chopsticks. Ghosn was totally preoccupied with problems surrounding the implementation of the NRP. But Tsuji continued to instruct him in a very patient manner. Ghosn tried to follow his instructions but he kept dropping food.

Later in his office Ghosn's secretary brought him a package from Tsuji. Inside the package was a description with photographs of the proper way to hold chopsticks. At first Ghosn stared at the pictures in disbelief. There were executives pounding on his door with news of one crisis after another. Nissan was sliding deeper into debt with the mounting costs of restructuring. People were not moving quickly enough to implement the changes, and Ghosn was faced with the prospect of issuing a profit warning. All he could think about was how they were going to get the company back on its feet. Yet there in front of him on the desk were pictures with detailed instructions on the proper technique of using chopsticks.

Upon reflection Ghosn realized that, though he may not have known it, Tsuji was giving Ghosn a lesson in life. No matter what the problems are that you must face each day, you cannot forget the small things. Holding the chopsticks correctly was necessary if Ghosn hoped to make a good impression on Japanese subordinates and colleagues.

The lesson reminded Ghosn of the importance of even the tiniest facets of managing a company. You cannot ignore them, just as you cannot ignore the proper way of holding chopsticks.

- Do not ignore the small things. Some things may appear to be insignificant, but there is a lesson to be learned from even the smallest thing.

"Ghosn can be found where it hurts. Wherever the problem is. That is where the president should be."

Key events in the life of Carlos Ghosn

1954	Born in Porto Velho, Brazil
1960	Entered Notre Dame Jesuit school in Lebanon
1974	Received chemical engineering degree from the École Polytechnique in Paris
1978	Graduated from the École des Mines in Paris and joined Michelin
1981	Appointed plant manager at Le Puy, France
1985	Moved to Brazil as Chief Operating Officer, Michelin Brazil
1989	Appointed President of Michelin's North American operations and moved to Greenville, South Carolina, USA
1990	Named Chairman, President and Chief Executive Officer of Michelin North America Inc.
1996	Left Michelin to become Executive Vice President of the Renault Group
1999	Renault S.A. bought 36.8 percent stock in Nissan and Ghosn moved to Tokyo as Chief Operating Officer and Representative Director of Nissan Motor Co., Ltd.
2001	Appointed President and Chief Executive Officer of Nissan Motor Co., Ltd.
2002	Ghosn appointed Director, Alcoa Inc., Director, Renault S.A.
2003	Nissan posted a group operating profit of 737.2 billion yen, up 51 percent
2004	Nissan posted a group operating profit of 860 billion yen and attained an operating margin of over 10 percent, making it the highest among volume automakers; Ghosn appointed Director, IBM
2005	Ghosn appointed CEO of the Renault Group effective May 1, 2005, thus making him CEO of both Renault S.A. and Nissan Motor Co., Ltd.

Sources

Interviews, *Kyodo News*, Economic News Section, Japan Spotlight, May/June 2004; *Weekly Toyo Keizai*, July 26, 2003; *Toyo Keizai*, May 15, 2004; *Nikkei Sangyo Newspaper*, 50th anniversary edition, five-part series, October 15–21, 2003.

BusinessWeek, Asian Edition, October 4, 2004.

Speeches: at Cranfield University, November 28, 2002; for the Japan Management Association, February 19, 2003; for the Japan Dealers Association, February 21, 2003; for (Japan's) National Town Hall Meeting, March 16, 2003; for the Business Conference in Cairo, Egypt, July 8, 2003; for the ACI World Congress, Lebanon, September 13, 2003; for the Yale Leaders Forum Lecture, Working effectively across cultures, November 12, 2003; for the JIJI Press Research Institute of Japan, May 31, 2004; for Leadership 1-1-1, Keidanran Kaikan, Tokyo, November 1, 2004.

Press conference, Nissan 180 and Fiscal Year 2003 Review, April 26, 2004.

Carlos Ghosn, "Opinion Leader" column, *American Chamber of Commerce Journal*, December 2003; "Making Changes to Create Value", article in the *Bungei Shunju Magazine*, November 10, 2004.

Carlos Ghosn with Miguel Rivas-Micoud and Kermit J. Carvell. *Renaissance* (Tokyo: Diamond Inc., 2001).

Peter F. Drucker as told to Miguel Rivas-Micoud, *Diamond Harvard Business Review*, November and December 2003 issues.

Author's interviews and conversations with Carlos Ghosn.

The McGraw-Hill Professional Education Series

How to Manage Performance: 24 Lessons for Improving Performance
   By Robert Bacal (0-07-143531-X)
   Goal-focused, commonsense techniques for stimulating greater productivity in the workplace and fostering true commitment.

Dealing with Difficult People: 24 Lessons for Bringing Out the Best in Everyone
   By Rick Brinkman and Rick Kirschner (0-07-141641-2)
   Learn about the 10 types of problem people and how to effectively respond to them to improve communication and collaboration.

How to Motivate Every Employee: 24 Proven Tactics to Spark Productivity in the Workplace
   By Anne Bruce (0-07-141333-2)
   By a master motivator and speaker, this book quickly reviews practical ways you can turn on employees and enhance their performance and your own.

Six Sigma for Managers: 24 Lessons to Understand and Apply Six Sigma Principles in Any Organization
   By Greg Brue (0-07-145548-5)
   Introduces the fundamental concepts of Six Sigma and details practical steps to spearhead a Six Sigma program in the workplace.

How to Be a Great Coach: 24 Lessons for Turning on the Productivity of Every Employee
   By Marshall J. Cook (0-07-143529-8)
   Today's most effective coaching methods to dramatically improve the performance of your employees.

Leadership When the Heat's On: 24 Lessons in High Performance Management
   By Danny Cox and John Hoover (0-07-141406-1)
   Learn hands-on techniques for infusing any company with results-driven leadership at every level, especially during times of organizational turmoil.

Networking for Career Success: 24 Lessons for Getting to Know the Right People
   By Diane Darling (0-07-145603-1)
   Learn the steps for making mutually beneficial career connections and the know-how to cultivate those connections for the benefit of everyone involved.

Why Customers Don't Do What You Want Them To: 24 Solutions to Common Selling Problems
By Ferdinand Fournies (0-07-141750-8)
This results-focused guidebook will help you to recognize and resolve 20 common selling problems and objections and help you move beyond them.

The Powell Principles: 24 Lessons from Colin Powell, a Legendary Leader
By Oren Harari (0-07-141109-7)
Colin Powell's success as a leader is universally acknowledged. Quickly learn his approach to leadership and the methods he uses to move people and achieve goals.

Project Management: 24 Lessons to Help You Master Any Project
By Gary Heerkens (0-07-145087-4)
An overview for first-time project managers that details what's expected of them and how to quickly get the lay of the land.

The Welch Way: 24 Lessons from the World's Greatest CEO
By Jeffrey A. Krames (0-07-138750-1)
Quickly learn some of the winning management practices that made Jack Welch one of the most successful CEOs ever.

The Lombardi Rules: 26 Lessons from Vince Lombardi—the World's Greatest Coach
By Vince Lombardi, Jr. (0-07-141108-9)
A quick course on the rules of leadership behind Coach Vince Lombardi and how anyone can use them to achieve extraordinary results.

Making Teams Work: 24 Lessons for Working Together Successfully
By Michael Maginn (0-07-143530-1)
Guidelines for molding individual team members into a solid, functioning group.

Managing in Times of Change: 24 Tools for Managers, Individuals, and Teams
By Michael Maginn (0-07-144911-6)
Straight talk and actionable advice on making sure that any manager, team, or individual moves through change successfully.

Persuasive Proposals and Presentations: 24 Lessons for Writing Winners
By Heather Pierce (0-07-145089-0)
A short, no-nonsense approach to writing proposals and presentations that sell.

The Sales Success Handbook: 20 Lessons to Open and Close Sales Now
By Linda Richardson (0-07-141636-6)
Learn how the consultative selling approach makes everyone in the transaction a winner. Close more sales and create long-term relationships with customers.

The New Manager's Handbook: 24 Lessons for Mastering Your New Role
   By Morey Stettner (0-07-141334-0)
   Here are 24 quick, sensible, and easy-to-implement practices to help new managers succeed from day one.

Finance for Non-Financial Managers: 24 Lessons to Understand and Evaluate Financial Health
   By Katherine Wagner (0-07-145090-4)
   This guide offers a bundle of lessons to clearly explain financial issues in lay terms.

Getting Organized at Work: 24 Lessons to Set Goals, Establish Priorities, and Manage Your Time
   By Kenneth Zeigler (0-07-145779-8)
   Supplies tips, tools, ideas, and strategies for becoming more organized with work tasks and priorities in order to get more done in less time.

The Handbook for Leaders: 24 Lessons for Extraordinary Leadership
   By John H. Zenger and Joseph Folkman (0-07-143532-8)
   A workplace-tested prescription for encouraging the behaviors and key drivers of effective leadership, from one of today's top training teams.